Overcoming the Power of Lust

Road to Victory

Bill Vincent

Overcoming the Power of Lust

© 2016 by Bill Vincent.
All rights reserved. No part of this book may be reproduced, stored in a retrieval system or transmitted in any form or by any means without the prior written permission of the publishers, except by a reviewer who may quote brief passages in a review to be printed in a newspaper, magazine or journal.

Softcover 978-1-60796-979-2

PUBLISHED BY REVIVAL WAVES OF GLORY BOOKS & PUBLISHING
www.revivalwavesofgloryministries.com
Litchfield, IL

Printed in the United States of America

Table of Contents

Introduction 4
Chapter One Removing LUST 5
Chapter Two Spiritual Suicide 11
Chapter Three Lust of the Flesh 13
Chapter Four Secret Lusts 20
Chapter Five Satan, the Great Counterfeiter 22
Chapter Six The Word Is Never Done 24
Chapter Seven Call No Man Father 27
Chapter Eight Lust for Position and Power 32
Chapter Nine Satan, Sin, and Seduction 34
Chapter Ten Deceptive Desires 39
Chapter Eleven No Respect 45
Chapter Twelve Protection From False Desires 51
About the Author 54
Recommended Books 56

Introduction

This book has been put together to help the Body of Christ discover their Road to Victory concerning the power of lust. Bill Vincent has personally helped hundreds to be free from this powerful spiritual battle. Lust is also linked to people's evil desires and greed related to materialism and self-gratification. *OVERCOMING THE POWER OF LUST is an easy read of a Bible based strategy to finding victory.* Lust is not only slipping its ways of perversion into the house of the Lord, but also into society everywhere. Pornography is destroying lives, homes, and marriages, which are falling apart every minute. You are sure to *OVERCOME THE POWER OF LUST* as you find your road to victory.

Chapter One
Removing LUST

I want to start this book by releasing some powerful keys to Remove LUST.

Galatians 5:16, 17 *This* I say then, Walk in the Spirit, and ye shall not fulfil the lust of the flesh. For the flesh lusteth against the Spirit, and the Spirit against the flesh: and these are contrary the one to the other: so that ye cannot do the things that ye would.

Titus 2:11, 12 For the grace of God that bringeth salvation hath appeared to all men, Teaching us that, denying ungodliness and worldly lusts, we should live soberly, righteously, and godly, in this present world;

As we keep living life and grow older, we are surrounded with diverse kinds of temptations. Believers have to be prepared and equipped when *lust* and *fantasy lust* come their way. *Lust* is defined in two different ways:

1. Strong sexual and sensual desire toward another person

2. Intense longing for something (like power or control)

Lust

Unifies

Sex and

Temptations

As we study the Word of the Lord, we will notice that, from Genesis to Revelation, lust is not merely sexual. Lust is also linked to people's evil desires and greed related to materialism and self-gratification.

James 1:14, 15 But every man is tempted, when he is drawn away of his own lust, and enticed. Then when lust hath conceived, it bringeth forth sin: and sin, when it is finished, bringeth forth death.

Scripture tells us that we must come against and cast down these kinds of thoughts and actions in our everyday living.

2Corinthians 10:5 Casting down imaginations, and every high thing that exalteth itself against the knowledge of God, and bringing into captivity every thought to the obedience of Christ;

The association of *lust* with sexual behaviors has been amplified in the Church and the world. Lust is not only slipping its ways of perversion into the house of the Lord, but also into society everywhere. Pornography is destroying lives, homes, and marriages, which are falling apart every minute.

2Timothy 3:1-5 This know also, that in the last days perilous times shall come. For men shall be lovers of their own selves, covetous, boasters, proud, blasphemers, disobedient to parents, unthankful, unholy, Without natural affection, trucebreakers, false accusers, incontinent, fierce, despisers of those that are good, Traitors, heady, highminded, lovers of pleasures more than lovers of God; Having a form of godliness, but denying the power thereof: from such turn away.

Now this spirit is overflowing into our young people, the saved and the unsaved, the churchgoer and the non-churchgoer. They all are arriving in a harmful arena, knowing they will never return from their fornications and wicked deeds *chiefly* because their consciences are seared.

2Timothy 3:8 Now as Jannes and Jambres withstood Moses, so do these also resist the truth: men of corrupt minds, reprobate concerning the faith.

The Lord God has designed since the beginning of time for us to stay away from *all* kinds of sensual, sexual, and lustful sins. Lust is one of the deadliest aspects of our sinful nature, alongside wickedness. When lust and debauchery (wickedness) are united, they contain the power to open us up to various kinds of spirits, demons, the spirit of Delilah, pornography, the spirit of Potiphar's wife, and Belial. These spirits have the power spiritually and physically to overpower us, causing mental slavery. Only the Holy Spirit and the anointing can break the tyranny over our lives!

Those who have been overcome by any of these malicious spirits— and they do work as a team—will need a man or woman of God anointed with a powerful deliverance ministry to assist in breaking the cycles of generational curses and familiar spirits that such people may have invited into their inner circle. Deliverance is needed in order to be made free from these types of strongholds; this is very vital in the lives of believers. This enticement of immorality is very powerful. Like a drug, it takes people into a world of false hopes and dreams. Society as a whole is collapsing right in front of us because of this, and we have no idea how to stop it. But we serve a God who holds everything in the power of His Name. Here is Heaven's strategy:

- First, war against it with the spirit of prayer.
- Second, defeat the enemy by not taking part in his false endeavors.
- Third, fast for what is good and abstain from evil desires of all sorts.

The lifestyle of promiscuity (behavior characterized by casual and indiscriminate sexual intercourse, often with many people) and distorted views of sex are running this great country of ours down to total destruction—in the natural as well as in the spiritual. Corrupt mentalities, combined with strong lustful envy, have created a wicked culture consumed with pornography, which has evolved into a multi-billion dollar a year industry, surpassing alcohol and drugs combined. Lechery (Excessive or offensive sexual desire; lustfulness) is a powerful weapon that we have pursued in our flesh and our souls without giving ear to the many consequences, which are very significant.

As the years have gone by, the Church has stopped speaking about these issues because of the explicit nature and graphic content of it.

Hosea 4:6 My people are destroyed for lack of knowledge: because thou hast rejected knowledge, I will also reject thee, that thou shalt be no priest to me: seeing thou hast forgotten the law of thy God, I will also forget thy children.

However, it is so critical in the days we are living in. Saints have to be transformed mentally according to the well-timed Scriptures the apostle Paul wrote about in Romans:

Romans 12:1, 2 I beseech you therefore, brethren, by the mercies of God, that ye present your bodies a living sacrifice, holy, acceptable unto God, *which is* your reasonable service. And be not conformed to this world: but be ye transformed by the renewing of your mind, that ye may prove what *is* that good, and acceptable, and perfect, will of God.

Chapter Two
Spiritual Suicide

It is time for all of us to realize the enemy always wants us to destroy ourselves with our own desires. Demons do not force us to fall into the hands of a Jezebel spirit; we invite it in by a willing heart. Sometimes believers will say things like, "The devil made me do it," or "I couldn't help it, the temptation was just too strong to fight off." There's a fine line between an excuse and a person who is willing to sin. Reality is, such people have been entertaining the images and thoughts that entered the theatres of their minds without taking into consideration that they are suppose to cast those iniquitous mental movies down:

2Corinthians 10:5, 6 Casting down imaginations, and every high thing that exalteth itself against the knowledge of God, and bringing into captivity every thought to the obedience of Christ; And having in a readiness to revenge all disobedience, when your obedience is fulfilled.

If an image comes into our minds, we have approximately less than three seconds to cast it down before it gets to our hearts. Once it gets into our souls—our hearts—it is too late. We are already ensnared by the wicked deceitfulness of your own desires.

Jeremiah 17:9 The heart *is* deceitful above all *things,* and desperately wicked: who can know it?

Chapter Three
Lust of the Flesh

Nowhere in Scripture do we find a demonic spirit of lust explicitly named, though many passages mention lust. There are many spirits that are associated but lust itself is within the persons flesh.

Romans 6:12 Let not sin therefore reign in your mortal body, that ye should obey it in the lusts thereof.

James 1:14 But every man is tempted, when he is drawn away of his own lust, and enticed.

Enticed means to: attract with pleasure and reward. Written by the apostles to caution the Body of Christ, the purpose of these verses was to instruct us how to prevent sin from reigning in our mortal bodies and, therefore, prevent us from obeying lust.

1John 2:16 For all that *is* in the world, the lust of the flesh, and the lust of the eyes, and the pride of life, is not of the Father, but is of the world.

We fight it with Scripture, consecration, quotes of warfare, prayer, and fasting—these are the keys to overcoming this entire ordeal. Lust opens doors to the evil spirit named *Belial;* all kinds of perverted spirits are under his authority. He sends them to tempt us, but no spirits come into us to force us to fall into sin—unless they are willingly invited. Distorted sexual views and openness will unlock spiritual portals that will be hard to close. Evil spirits will physically and spiritually destroy us and keep us longer than we ever intended. When they are done with us, we will be dead! We must fall on our faces in the sight of God in these evil days, as it gets darker and darker by the minute.

So many movies and television shows contain vulgar words that were never allowed when I was a child; now they are televised with no conscience or ethics. Sex and vulgarity are being amplified and exhibited graphically; we must work harder than ever to filter these things so our children don't have to hear and see the perversion of the world's social disorder.

The Lord has made a way for Christians to take the Word of God and run with zeal for the

Good News of Christ in order to protect the moral values that we have left. We must take holiness and purity by force immediately, or we will stumble before the King of kings! As living sacrifices, we have to deny ourselves when it comes to our evil desires and wants. The Spirit of the Lord will help and guide us *if* we call on His Name. We are living in a desperate and chaotic age, but God has a plan to redeem and refresh us all in the near future. Hanging on to what is good is the duty of all those who are saved and Holy Ghost-filled. We must endure until the end and fight with wisdom so that we may experience the refreshing that is coming. We must be ready always and fight our flesh until the end, and we will be rewarded.

1Corinthians 10:12, 13 Wherefore let him that thinketh he standeth take heed lest he fall. There hath no temptation taken you but such as is common to man: but God *is* faithful, who will not suffer you to be tempted above that ye are able; but will with the temptation also make a way to escape, that ye may be able to bear *it*.

Authentic Christians must want the relief only Christ can give in order to walk in liberty.

The Holy Spirit will see we are serious. If we hold true, He will start to burn in us like a fire within our members—captivating our minds and souls with faithfulness, making us complete and whole on the inside. He will cause us to put a halt on our cravings that are contradictory to God's laws and His mental map of holiness so that we can walk in His freedom. This is who we are in the Lord. It's Christ who rewards us openly, operating in and satisfying the empty and the fallen. Feeling like a failure, yet we are successful; having conflict and disruption on all sides, yet we have a battle cry on reserve. Let's adjust ourselves and be prepared. Lust will constantly knock on the doors of our hearts, but when it does knock, we have to let it knock and never answer.

(No matter how many times we say *no*, it will still knock on occasion because we are still incased in flesh.)

Singles who are sexually frustrated must go above and beyond what is expected. Jesus will always be there to give you the strength that you need, enabling you to do all things through Him. Depend on God with all of your might!

Philippians 4:8, 9 Finally, brethren, whatsoever things are true, whatsoever things *are* honest, whatsoever things *are* just, whatsoever things *are* pure, whatsoever things *are* lovely, whatsoever things *are* of good report; if *there be* any virtue, and if *there be* any praise, think on these things. Those things, which ye have both learned, and received, and heard, and seen in me, do: and the God of peace shall be with you.

Philippians 4:13 I can do all things through Christ which strengtheneth me.

Ephesians 6:10 Finally, my brethren, be strong in the Lord, and in the power of his might.

God promises that you don't have to do it in your own power.

Zechariah 4:6 Then he answered and spake unto me, saying, This *is* the word of the LORD unto Zerubbabel, saying, Not by might, nor by power, but by my spirit, saith the LORD of hosts.

He has provided your way of escape. The Lord will be Lord forever—that is His name! You can't overcome lust without God. He is the King who will reign eternally, and His decrees and mannerisms are from everlasting to everlasting. After dissecting the plans of the enemy in order to know our true purpose in our lives, the gift of infinity will not be given to us if we fall into the company of evil desires and camp there. The angels called Goodness and Mercy our stepping-stones, following us throughout our years, like they once did for David of the Old Testament.

Psalms 23:6 Surely goodness and mercy shall follow me all the days of my life: and I will dwell in the house of the LORD for ever.

Some time ago I tried to amend myself with my own authority, trying to set myself free, not knowing that freedom from bondage comes only through the influence of Jesus' Spirit.

Psalms 34:19 Many *are* the afflictions of the righteous: but the LORD delivereth him out of them all.

Now I know to take comfort in His existence, which is above all. Righteous people who encounter concupiscence, or strong sexual desire, must learn to deflect lust through the influence of God's Spirit of purity, who resists depraved ambitions, whether sexual or not. We must surround ourselves with the presence of the Lord above; an exciting spirit will be subject to the Spirit of Christ, who can never co-exist with evil when sitting on the right side of the throne of power in our hearts! All born again believers who have their names written in the Lamb's Book of Life are seated in heavenly places. Glory to God! No matter what we face, God promises us:

Ephesians 2:6, 7 And hath raised *us* up together, and made *us* sit together in heavenly *places* in Christ Jesus: That in the ages to come he might shew the exceeding riches of his grace in *his* kindness toward us through Christ Jesus.

James 4:7, 8 Submit yourselves therefore to God. Resist the devil, and he will flee from you. Draw nigh to God, and he will draw nigh to you. Cleanse *your* hands, *ye* sinners; and purify *your* hearts, *ye* double minded.

Chapter Four

Secret Lusts

Lust is out to destroy as many as possible. Lust was a downfall for one of the greatest Kings who ever walked the face of the earth, King David, the prophet of the Great God Yahweh. From his palace, King David watched Bathsheba, another man's wife, as she was taking a *bath*. Not only did he watch, but he gave into his yearning for Bathsheba, eventually making her pregnant. Afterward, he contemplated within himself how he would kill Bathsheba's husband, Uriah the Hittite, so that he could have her. Using his power wrongly fed the dark abyss of his own lust, and he misused his authority to deceive in order to get what he wickedly desired. When he did receive what he craved, it was more than he could bear. David learned his lesson; it was a very difficult trail for him to walk on.

The story of Samson and Delilah is an account in the Bible of betrayal between two consenting adults who were engulfed with not the same passion for each other for the wrong reasons. Samson lusted after Delilah because of her beauty, and Delilah lusted after Samson because greed for 1,100 pieces of silver (which were offered as a reward for Samson's capture) took over her.

Judges 16:4, 5 And it came to pass afterward, that he loved a woman in the valley of Sorek, whose name *was* **Delilah. And the lords of the Philistines came up unto her, and said unto her, Entice him, and see wherein his great strength** *lieth,* **and by what** *means* **we may prevail against him, that we may bind him to afflict him: and we will give thee every one of us eleven hundred** *pieces* **of silver.**

Needless to say, the Bible points out countless others who fell in a similar snare because of greed, lust, and a desire for control. Nonetheless, God has proven Himself faithful to all of His servants by modifying their lives into something great. God ultimately used Samson to destroy many Philistines (Israel's enemy), even while he was in bondage.

God loves to knock the devil off of his platform of pride and prevent him from driving the people of God into nothingness.

Chapter Five
Satan, the Great Counterfeiter

Satan is always making things look better than they really are. As we know, satan is the great counterfeiter; he will mimic his way into every tiny crack available to him, with the goal of making sure we follow hard after him, giving our lives to pride and false worship.

We must be very discerning and aware of his wicked ideas and false wonders. These terrible times are beginning to manifest his children in places and positions that we never thought possible. Pastors are turning into witches; bishops are turning into warlocks; false teaching is everywhere; false signs are more than ever. Ultimately, they are *all* counterfeits of evil and spirits of malice! Treacherous behavior will emerge, as a result, causing iniquity to enter into the hearts of multitudes around the planet. It's about to get darker, but at the same time, *God* will manifest

His power through His Light on earth—the Church!

Chapter Six
The Word Is Never Done

In the Old Testament prophets, we read of all the troubles they had to face, but they still held on to what was good for the Will of God. When we compare recorded events of the past with real life events of today, we see that there are equivalent issues that have been going on since the very beginning of time. The egotistic concepts and ideas in our times mirror deceptions from ages past. Solomon wrote that there is nothing new under the sun, and it is still true.

Ecclesiastes 1:9 The thing that hath been, it *is that* which shall be; and that which is done *is* that which shall be done: and *there is* no new *thing* under the sun.

After He takes us out of the fire and we are looking beautiful, even then He is not done with us. The work always continues until our change comes. God's ways are so divergent.

He desires for us to be transformed by the renewing of our minds so that we will stay that way.

Romans 12:1, 2 *I beseech you therefore, brethren, by the mercies of God, that ye present your bodies a living sacrifice, holy, acceptable unto God, which is your reasonable service. And be not conformed to this world: but be ye transformed by the renewing of your mind, that ye may prove what is that good, and acceptable, and perfect, will of God.*

Transformation is necessary to help us thwart the traps of satan and the lusts of our flesh and the world. Those who say that God is understanding of our wallowing in sin, that He will not allow judgment to be executed on our lives, are only self-deceived. Here is a warning that the apostle Paul wrote to the people of Galatia.

Galatians 5:16 *This I say then, Walk in the Spirit, and ye shall not fulfil the lust of the flesh.*

From Genesis to Revelation, we read about "the lust of the flesh" (not "the spirit of lust") and the damage it has caused all through history. Christ and the apostles understood this. The apostle Paul expressed it in Romans

7:14-21, detailing his personal struggles while being single.

Romans 7:14-21 For we know that the law is spiritual: but I am carnal, sold under sin. For that which I do I allow not: for what I would, that do I not; but what I hate, that do I. If then I do that which I would not, I consent unto the law that *it is* good. Now then it is no more I that do it, but sin that dwelleth in me. For I know that in me (that is, in my flesh,) dwelleth no good thing: for to will is present with me; but *how* to perform that which is good I find not. For the good that I would I do not: but the evil which I would not, that I do. Now if I do that I would not, it is no more I that do it, but sin that dwelleth in me. I find then a law, that, when I would do good, evil is present with me.

Chapter Seven
Call No Man Father

God showed me something concerning Catholic Priests and I thought wow we need to all see this. Lust, whether spiritual, soulish, or natural, is sin in the eyes of Christ. Consider this carefully:

Matthew 23:9 And call no *man* your father upon the earth: for one is your Father, which is in heaven.

He was not telling us to not call our natural dads, *father*; rather, I believe He foreknew that Catholic would arise after He ascended to His heavenly Father and He was addressing an error in that belief. In Catholic, a priest (who is called "father") goes into one side of a booth, and lay Catholics enter the opposite side of the same booth. A dialogue ensues between them, resulting in private confessions of all types, including sinful activities that the lay person has committed. These confessions always culminate with the request of the priest, "Father, forgive me for I have sinned." After years and years of known and unknown members confessing their sins to the priest, a transformation begins to take place in the soul and spirit of the priest, most times unknowingly. Opening the ear gate of the soul for years, listening to admissions of sin and vulgar behavior can quickly destroy a life in many ways.

Jesus plainly said, "Don't confess your sins to mere people because they are just that—people. They don't have the authority or the supremacy to forgive us, nor are they able to wash our sins away and repel the weight of sin"

Mark 2:7 Why doth this *man* thus speak blasphemies? who can forgive sins but God only?

If we ponder what Jesus said, we will see that it makes total and complete sense. Confessing all kinds of sins, lies, lust issues, and everything under the sun will put a priest to his knees; opening portals to satanic oppression (keep in mind that most Catholic priests are not born-again Christians). Here is the result of this religious process; we see them on the news for molestation, rape, or sodomy charges—sometimes all of the above. I am sure somewhere in our country and in our world it's happening; we are not to be naïve of that fact, but it's not as frequent or as televised. If a pastor or anyone in ministry is guilty of the same behavior in the presence of Christ, it will not go unpunished, even if it's not televised or in the morning paper. We have the Holy Spirit to convict us and guide us. God allows us to be married, in part so that our minds do not travel farther than our flesh should go.

Sadly, too often the Catholic priests are either expelled or excluded from the Vatican or the Catholic Church. When we realize the filth a Catholic father goes through, listening to the heaviness of sin, it becomes clear that priests do not have the capability to maintain a pure heart and mind before God in this environment.

Jeremiah 17:9 The heart *is* deceitful above all *things*, and desperately wicked: who can know it?

This is true because sin is a great burden to carry. The end result is that people (in this instance, priests) act out what has been poured into them. Countless priests have kept themselves from women, yet have different people from all walks of life visiting and confessing month after month and year after year their sexual immoralities. Eventually it will take a hold on them sexually. The sins of men are too heavy for a mere people to deal with. God has created us to be sexual beings, but in the confines of marriage and not in fornication and promiscuity. Lust is very powerful, especially when we feed it. Not everyone will act on every thought or devious behavior that enters their minds, but many will eventually act on some of those thoughts. We all must be clever to know the designs of the devil and how he is trying to destroy us. We must be aware of the enemy and know our true purpose.

1Corinthians 7:9 But if they cannot contain, let them marry: for it is better to marry than to burn.

Ephesians 4:17-24 This I say therefore, and testify in the Lord, that ye henceforth walk not as other Gentiles walk, in the vanity of their mind, Having the understanding darkened, being alienated from the life of God through the ignorance that is in them, because of the blindness of their heart: Who being past feeling have given themselves over unto lasciviousness, to work all uncleanness with greediness. But ye have not so learned Christ; If so be that ye have heard him, and have been taught by him, as the truth is in Jesus: That ye put off concerning the former conversation the old man, which is corrupt according to the deceitful lusts; And be renewed in the spirit of your mind; And that ye put on the new man, which after God is created in righteousness and true holiness.

Chapter Eight
Lust for Position and Power

Many Catholic's consider Peter to be the first Pope (which is a prominent Catholic teaching) has confused millions of people, knowing that Popes have no dealings with women or marriage. Yet Peter had a mother-in-law, and the only way he could have a mother-in-law was if he was married to the daughter,

Luke 4:38 And he arose out of the synagogue, and entered into Simon's house. And Simon's wife's mother was taken with a great fever; and they besought him for her.

This shows how people take the Scriptures out of context and distort the true character and nature out of the Word, misconstruing what the Lord was trying to relay to humankind. Misinterpretation can be a very powerful arsenal, if we are not careful. This coincides in the same characteristics of Christianity and the Bible. We must make sure how we live and everything we teach is according to the Word of God for purity and righteousness. We often misinterpret the signs of sexual promiscuity and perversion. We have to be wise beyond our years, read our Bibles, and spend lots of time with God in prayer. Think of prayer as "powerful resources at our earliest request":

Philippians 4:6, 7 Be careful for nothing; but in every thing by prayer and supplication with thanksgiving let your requests be made known unto God. And the peace of God, which passeth all understanding, shall keep your hearts and minds through Christ Jesus.

Chapter Nine
Satan, Sin, and Seduction

We all have a sinful nature Satan wants to stir up. The one thing I can say with certainty is that there is victory if we are obedient and willing to follow hard after God, despite the problems stirring in the very apex of your intelligence. Many of us know better, yet we keep dabbling in sin and its nature. This should not be so. We must consecrate ourselves and give our all to the Lord Jesus Christ, without turning back, like the wife of Lot, when she turned into a pillar of salt.

Genesis 19:26 But his wife looked back from behind him, and she became a pillar of salt.

She looked back, which was a metaphoric sign of the attitude, "I don't want to start afresh; I miss my old life." This attitude violates this principle from Luke:

Luke 9:62 And Jesus said unto him, No man, having put his hand to the plough, and looking back, is fit for the kingdom of God.

The leading of the Spirit of Christ will enable us to make it. Let's tell our friends—a sister, a brother, saved or unsaved—that they can make it as long as they have the Spirit of Life within them. Satan is a liar and the father of lies.

John 8:44 Ye are of *your* father the devil, and the lusts of your father ye will do. He was a murderer from the beginning, and abode not in the truth, because there is no truth in him. When he speaketh a lie, he speaketh of his own: for he is a liar, and the father of it.

Whether we lust after material things, control, authority, power, or sexual pleasures, unless we deal with it quickly, we will be shaken and shattered. Believers must adhere to the Word and the Lord's commandments and stay away from satan's craftiness; he is constantly releasing snares to captivate us with impious seductions. I have seen worldly people right along with Christians fall on their faces quickly because of lust; at other times, it happens slowly. But the devil will make sure it happens, guaranteed! Evil spirits know who we are and whether we are really serving the Lord or just being counterfeit. They are very daring and will expose us, if we prove to be false, to those around us. Look at this account from the early Church:

Acts 19:11-16 And God wrought special miracles by the hands of Paul: So that from his body were brought unto the sick handkerchiefs or aprons, and the diseases departed from them, and the evil spirits went out of them. Then certain of the vagabond Jews, exorcists, took upon them to call over them which had evil spirits the name of the Lord Jesus, saying, We adjure you by Jesus whom Paul preacheth. And there were seven sons of *one* Sceva, a Jew, *and* chief of the priests, which did so. And the evil spirit answered and said, Jesus I know, and Paul I know; but who are ye? And the man in whom the evil spirit was leaped on them, and overcame them, and prevailed against them, so that they fled out of that house naked and wounded.

In years of ministry, I have witnessed first hand what it means when someone tries to *mock* the ways of God, thinking that they alone have the power to rebuke devils without knowing who Jesus is. The passage above proves beyond any reason that if you are not in an intimate relationship with the Lord, devils will not recognize who you are, therefore having access to hurt you in the process. If we don't take this seriously, demons will have a field day in our thought lives. They will bombard us with all kinds of miscellaneous temptations; graphic images will be displayed in our minds to knock us off track.

2Corinthians 3:17 Now the Lord is that Spirit: and where the Spirit of the Lord *is,* there *is* liberty.

John 8:36 If the Son therefore shall make you free, ye shall be free indeed.

Galatians 5:1 Stand fast therefore in the liberty wherewith Christ hath made us free, and be not entangled again with the yoke of bondage.

There is a big difference between being *set free* and *made free*. Allow me to paint a picture of the differences between the two. Being *set free* is when inmates, who are locked up in jail cells, are released; yet they are still behind bars of pure bondage in their hearts, minds, and spirits, even while their bodies are experiencing freedom. Being *made free* is when people receive Christ as Lord and Savior; they will experience liberty whether locked behind bars or not because the anointing destroys the yoke of mental and spiritual slavery. This allows anyone to experience genuine freedom with joy.

John 8:36 If the Son therefore shall make you free, ye shall be free indeed.

This is the true liberation of Christ. So let's walk audaciously and not in weakness.

Chapter Ten
Deceptive Desires

In all of this, we must pray that the Body of Christ would understand the precise characteristics of the Son of Man, who walked a short journey with his soul and body, but made camp in the Spirit. The Lord is magnificent and holy, unable to be explained infinite language. Yet we must make Jesus' ways known. Allowing lust and its relatives to reside in our members is not a wise choice to make.

From my point of view and the understanding I have gained of lust, I know it will take people to places from which it will be impossible to return. I drank alcohol, drugs, but lust was my worst drug, and it was bad. Trouble after trouble marching slowly in a desert of counterfeit desires will kill us!

Lust will always want more and more—*Just one more look* or *Just one more second*. Those thoughts are deceptions of the flesh and the devil. With his bow in hand, the enemy plays archery contests in our minds, seeing who will win—us or him. For men, such troubles are many; but it's the Lord who delivers us out of them all.

Psalms 34:6 This poor man cried, and the LORD heard *him,* and saved him out of all his troubles.

There are lewd thoughts and the workings that follow after. We men must take heed to these instructions for they are the life on the line for our souls.

John 10:7 Then said Jesus unto them again, Verily, verily, I say unto you, I am the door of the sheep.

Thoughts are very transparent and vague at times, but mostly enlightening. Allow me to explain. Not every thought that invites itself into our mental souls is ours. Having discernment and wisdom, according to the Spirit of God, is very critical in the Christian life so that we can counterattack evil thoughts with the Word. When thoughts rise up into our minds, sometimes it's just us; at other times, it's our enemy with his fiery darts, causing us to be interrupted and disrupted in our thought process. The Bible talks about satan as having flaming or fiery darts, which cause burning and heated thoughts.

Ephesians 6:10 Finally, my brethren, be strong in the Lord, and in the power of his might.

Let's say the thought was a negative one. We will always hear the right "thought voice"—the Holy Spirit—speak to us first. The Word tells us how to discern God's voice:

Jeremiah 29:10 For thus saith the LORD, That after seventy years be accomplished at Babylon I will visit you, and perform my good word toward you, in causing you to return to this place.

Then the wrong one enters immediately after. But the second "thought voice" usually sounds much louder than the first. The second thought is always the one that wants us to do an act of evil or say something that is unfruitful and not acceptable in the ears of God or others. The second voice contradicts the first on a regular basis. As these thoughts go in and out of our minds, we need to discern them quickly and wisely. If they exalt themselves against the knowledge of God and His Word, we must cast them down immediately. In our world, we have seen hundreds, maybe thousands, of men and women, even children, act on their thoughts, and the results were clearly devastating. Multitudes of believers in these last days can tell the difference—whether it's God or the devil talking to them. Our "thought voices" are our own, and we must be scrupulous at all times. In essence, we have to be aware of the content of our thoughts and what kind of information is being deposited into us. We must know how to become one with God and hear His still small voice so that when the Shepherd speaks there is no confusion in the process.

Prophetic people of God, hear the Holy Spirit's voice most of the time audibly on the outside and occasionally from the inside. It is not the same for everyone, but rarely does the Church feel impressed in it's spirit when God speaks; usually the Church literally hears His still small voice, which is not their own thought voice, and that is awesome!

We must re-tune and quiet ourselves away from all the noise that surrounds us—the Lord will speak to us. This is what happened with the prophet Elijah:

1Kings 19:11-13 And he said, Go forth, and stand upon the mount before the LORD. And, behold, the LORD passed by, and a great and strong wind rent the mountains, and brake in pieces the rocks before the LORD; *but* the LORD *was* not in the wind: and after the wind an earthquake; *but* the LORD *was* not in the earthquake: And after the earthquake a fire; *but* the LORD *was* not in the fire: and after the fire a still small voice. And it was *so*, when Elijah heard *it*, that he wrapped his face in his mantle, and went out, and stood in the entering in of the cave. And, behold, *there came* a voice unto him, and said, What doest thou here, Elijah?

The devil uses our own thought voices so we can be swindled, making it extremely difficult for us to determine who is speaking to us. If the devil used his supernatural voice, we would flip and go crazy because of the way his voice would sound; it would blow his cover and prevent us from implementing what he instructed. This would frustrate his evil plans and reveal his trickery. But if he can camouflage his voice with our own voices (if we do not have discernment), it could open a gateway of immeasurable evil in our lives; this is satan's primary objective—deception. Generally, most people, whether they serve the Lord or not, do not have this kind of understanding in order to detect destructive thinking. Consequently, they follow after and speak whatever enters their hearts; their thoughts simply flow out of their mouths, which we call blurting, offensive, and disrespectful speech. This can become dangerous for those who don't have close relationship with Christ to know the difference between their own thoughts and the enemy's voice.

Jesus said that out of the abundance of the heart the mouth will speak.

Luke 6:45 A good man out of the good treasure of his heart bringeth forth that which is good; and an evil man out of the evil treasure of his heart bringeth forth that which is evil: for of the abundance of the heart his mouth speaketh.

Proverbs 23:7 For as he thinketh in his heart, so *is* he: Eat and drink, saith he to thee; but his heart *is* not with thee.

We must be careful what thoughts we allow in our minds because they will determine our actions. If we dwell on and engage the enemy's evil imaginations, we will eventually obey his voice to our own demise.

Chapter Eleven
No Respect

I am tired of seeing men falling because of this powerful subject of LUST. Magnitudes of people around the world know firsthand what I am writing about. Satan is making sure we stay in a cloud of lustful cravings that can never be satisfied in order to bring us a pinnacle of disease and false dominance. Society and the world are always relating lust to sex, but it is also often associated with greed for power and control, though the general public tells us otherwise. This is a Jezebel spirit in its purest form under the influence of Belial, a demon general of satan's kingdom.

1Samuel 30:22 Then answered all the wicked men and *men* of Belial, of those that went with David, and said, Because they went not with us, we will not give them *ought* of the spoil that we have recovered, save to every man his wife and his children, that they may lead *them* away, and depart.

1Kings 21:13 And there came in two men, children of Belial, and sat before him: and the men of Belial witnessed against him, *even* against Naboth, in the presence of the people, saying, Naboth did blaspheme God and the king. Then they carried him forth out of the city, and stoned him with stones, that he died.

2Corinthians 6:15 And what concord hath Christ with Belial? or what part hath he that believeth with an infidel?

Relationship with worldliness and distorted views is adopted by fools at such a great rate that it's beyond comprehension to the natural realm. Belial and Jezebel are interrelated. We cannot take part at all with darkness. Sadly, many are yoked in spiritual slavery and don't even know it. We know better; we are supposed to be a light in a dark place and salt in a world that has lost its flavor.

Matthew 5:13 Ye are the salt of the earth: but if the salt have lost his savour, wherewith shall it be salted? it is thenceforth good for nothing, but to be cast out, and to be trodden under foot of men.

In our day, unsaved people can't tell the world from a Christian, because we all look and sound alike. Distinct change and godliness has to be the attribute of all the people of God; we are called to come out from among them and be separate.

2Corinthians 6:17 Wherefore come out from among them, and be ye separate, saith the Lord, and touch not the unclean *thing;* and I will receive you,

1Corinthians 9:22 To the weak became I as weak, that I might gain the weak: I am made all things to all *men,* that I might by all means save some.

To a certain degree we must become all things to all people to win some, that's very true. Yet, we must do this with the *leading* of the Holy Spirit, adhering to His counsel at all times, not the counsel of our theological degrees and head knowledge of the Word. As a peculiar people and a holy nation, we must keep in mind that satan does not respect the Bible, esteem holy reverence, or worship God. He knows the Bible better than we do, but does not respect it. When we only read the Word of God—apart from the Spirit—it is only words on a page; therefore, he does not respect the Word alone. He knows that the Kingdom of God is not in words, but in power. The devil respects and gives reverence to the Holy Spirit!

1Corinthians 4:20 For the kingdom of God *is* not in word, but in power.

Combine believers with the Word *and* the Spirit of Christ who is in us—the hope of all glory and *BAM*, satan will submit to our authority.

Colossians 1:27 To whom God would make known what *is* the riches of the glory of this mystery among the Gentiles; which is Christ in you, the hope of glory:

1John 5:21 Little children, keep yourselves from idols. Amen.

Until then, we must watch and pray and keep ourselves from idols. Idols can be anything we love more than God.

1. Children
2. Spouse
3. House
4. Car
5. Lust
6. Pornography
7. Ourselves

This is why we can't *always* become all things to all people. If I have idolized cars, I am deceived if I think I am buying a luxury car simply to "be all things to all people." No, I am just feeding my idol.

Such thinking apart from the Spirit leaves room for error and confusion. As the Word says:

2Corinthians 6:14, 15Be ye not unequally yoked together with unbelievers: for what fellowship hath righteousness with unrighteousness? and what communion hath light with darkness? And what concord hath Christ with Belial? or what part hath he that believeth with an infidel?

We must be careful at all times and not enter into situations without the Spirit of God ahead of us and with us. We have to walk in, walk with, and walk by the power of Christ's Spirit. There is no other way.

Deuteronomy 13:13-15 *Certain* men, the children of Belial, are gone out from among you, and have withdrawn the inhabitants of their city, saying, Let us go and serve other gods, which ye have not known; Then shalt thou enquire, and make search, and ask diligently; and, behold, *if it be* truth, *and* the thing certain, *that* such abomination is wrought among you; Thou shalt surely smite the inhabitants of that city with the edge of the sword, destroying it utterly, and all that *is* therein, and the cattle thereof, with the edge of the sword.

Chapter Twelve
Protection From False Desires

We need to have leaders in place for protection. Some pastors and ministers can tell the voice of the devil in a second, with no hesitation. Because they see that it is insidious and hurtful to their flocks, they will war and pray against that spirit to bring liberation. Since love and awareness rests on the mantle of their hearts, they also know firsthand that if some of their congregants have heard the real voice of our adversary (or if demons manifest from the spirit realm and physically touch these believers), fear will begin to prevail and deliverance must take place.

Jeremiah 3:15 And I will give you pastors according to mine heart, which shall feed you with knowledge and understanding.

Therefore, they will need the pastor, apostle, or elder to facilitate in overcoming any confusion and bringing understanding to that situation. I have a trained ear to know the distinction of the voice of God and the voice of the devil. We must know how to discern the voices to know if it's us, God, or the devil. Jesus said that His followers, His sheep, will know His voice and follow His voice rather than the voice of a stranger (the devil):

John 10:4, 5 And when he putteth forth his own sheep, he goeth before them, and the sheep follow him: for they know his voice. And a stranger will they not follow, but will flee from him: for they know not the voice of strangers.

John 10:27 My sheep hear my voice, and I know them, and they follow me:

There are many voices in our world today; mostly, those voices bring nothing but turmoil and tragedy. We must listen for only the Voice that brings redemption and beauty for ashes.

Isaiah 61:3 To appoint unto them that mourn in Zion, to give unto them beauty for ashes, the oil of joy for mourning, the garment of praise for the spirit of heaviness; that they might be called trees of righteousness, the planting of the LORD, that he might be glorified.

Overcoming the Power of Lust

You can become free if you allow the Holy Spirit to be your teacher. You are not alone God is with you.

About the Author

Bill Vincent is no stranger to understanding the power of God. Not only has he spent over twenty years as a Minister with a strong prophetic anointing, he is now also an Apostle and Author with Revival Waves of Glory Ministries in Litchfield, IL. Along with his wife, Tabitha, he, leads a team providing apostolic oversight in all aspects of ministry, including service, personal ministry and Godly character.

Bill offers a wide range of writings and teachings from deliverance, to experiencing presence of God and developing Apostolic cutting edge Church structure. Drawing on the power of the Holy Spirit through years of experience in Revival, Spiritual Sensitivity, and deliverance ministry, Bill now focuses mainly on pursuing the Presence of God and breaking the power of the devil off of people's lives.

His books 48 and counting has since helped many people to overcome the spirits and curses of Satan. For more information or to keep up with Bill's latest releases, please visit www.revivalwavesofgloryministries.com. To contact Bill, feel free to follow him on twitter @revivalwaves.

Recommended Books

By Bill Vincent
Overcoming Obstacles
Glory: Pursuing God's Presence
Defeating the Demonic Realm
Increasing Your Prophetic Gift
Increase Your Anointing
Keys to Receiving Your Miracle
The Supernatural Realm
Waves of Revival
Increase of Revelation and Restoration
The Resurrection Power of God
Discerning Your Call of God
Apostolic Breakthrough
Glory: Increasing God's Presence
Love is Waiting – Don't Let Love Pass You By
The Healing Power of God
Glory: Expanding God's Presence
Receiving Personal Prophecy
Signs and Wonders
Signs and Wonders Revelations
Children Stories
The Rapture
The Secret Place of God's Power
Building a Prototype Church
Breakthrough of Spiritual Strongholds
Glory: Revival Presence of God
Overcoming the Power of Lust
Glory: Kingdom Presence of God

Transitioning to the Prototype Church
The Stronghold of Jezebel
Healing After Divorce
A Closer Relationship With God
Cover Up and Save Yourself
Desperate for God's Presence
The War for Spiritual Battles
Spiritual Leadership
Global Warning
Millions of Churches
Destroying the Jezebel Spirit
Awakening of Miracles
Deception and Consequences Revealed
Are You a Follower of Christ
Don't Let the Enemy Steal from You!
A Godly Shaking
The Unsearchable Riches of Christ
Heaven's Court System
Satan's Open Doors
Armed for Battle
The Wrestler
Spiritual Warfare: Complete Collection
Growing In the Prophetic
Faith
The Angry Fighter's Story
Understanding Heaven's Court System

Web Site:
www.revivalwavesofgloryministries.com

www.ingramcontent.com/pod-product-compliance
Lightning Source LLC
Chambersburg PA
CBHW052121070526
44584CB00017B/2581